Hair Length in the Bible

Hair Length in the Bible

A Study of I Corinthians 11:2-16

DANIEL L. SEGRAVES

Hair Length in the Bible

A Study of I Corinthians 11:2-16

by Daniel L. Segraves

©1989 Word Aflame Press
Hazelwood, MO 63042-2299
Printing History: 1992, 1995, 1998, 2000, 2003

Cover Design by Paul Povolni

All Scripture quotations in this book are from the King James Version of the Bible unless otherwise identified.

All rights reserved. No portion of this publication may be reproduced, stored in an electronic system, or transmitted in any form or by any means, electronic, mechanical, photocopy, recording, or otherwise, without the prior permission of Word Aflame Press. Brief quotations may be used in literary reviews.

Printed in United States of America

WORD AFLAME®PRESS
8855 DUNN ROAD
HAZELWOOD, MO 63042-2299

www.pentecostalpublishing.com

Library of Congress Cataloging-in-Publication Data

Segraves, Daniel L., 1946–
   Hair length in the Bible : a study of I Corinthians 11:2–16 / Daniel L. Segraves.
      p.   cm.
   Rev. ed. of: Women's hair, the long and short of it. 1979.
   Includes bibliographical references.
   ISBN 0-932581-57-9 :
   1. Hairdressing—Biblical teaching. 2. Women—Biblical teaching.
3. Bible N.T. Corinthians, 1st. XI. 2-16—Criticism,
interpretation, etc. I. Segraves, Daniel L., 1946–   Women's hair.
the long and short of it. II. Title.
BS2675.6.H27   1989   89-37912
227'.2095—dc20   CIP

*To my wife,
who has indeed
been my glory*

(I Corinthians 11:7)

Contents

Preface
1. Introduction to I Corinthians 11:2-16 11
2. Analysis of I Corinthians 11:2-16 17
3. The Voice of History 49
4. Answers to Objections 57
5. The Letter and the Spirit 73

Preface

In 1979 I wrote the book *Women's Hair—The Long and Short of It*. The book came out of a desire to develop a personal certainty about the teaching of Scripture on that subject. The book was reprinted a number of times over the next ten years.

During this time I have continued to do research on the subject and to speak on it from time to time, primarily at the request of others. In 1986 I presented a paper on the subject at the first Symposium on Oneness Pentecostalism, and the paper was included in the book published from that symposium.

After a decade of having *Women's Hair* in print, I consulted with other ministers and determined that the time had come to completely rewrite and revise that first work. The result is this book.

This work, while taking the same basic position as the first, contains a great deal of additional information resulting from continued research. It is my prayer that it will benefit all who read it and that it will assist the reader in coming to a firm conclusion he can comfortably hold and conscientiously defend.

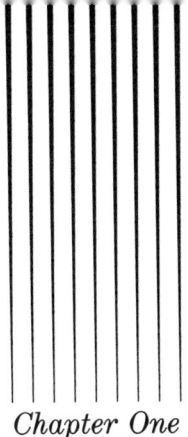

Chapter One

Introduction to I Corinthians 11:2-16

The clear teaching of the Bible regarding hair length for both men and women is found in I Corinthians 11:2-16, and our study will focus primarily on this passage. It is interesting to see how frequently current theological journals, magazines, and books discuss this text.[1] Most of the works agree that the passage speaks about a symbol that represents something far greater than itself. Disagreement arises as to whether the symbol is a material headdress or literal hair, and whether the symbol must be observed by the church today.

Most commentators agree that I Corinthians 11:2-16 falls within the portion of the epistle that makes up Paul's response to certain questions asked by the Corinthians. (See I Corinthians 7:1.) For example, David K. Lowery understands Paul to answer questions "on the topics of marriage (chap. 7), personal liberty (8:1-11:1), church order (11:2-14:40) and doctrine (chap. 15)."[2]

On the other hand, W. Harold Mare suggests that

Hair Length in the Bible

I Corinthians 11:2-16 is excluded from the larger section from 7:1 to 14:40 that is "devoted in a large part to answering questions."[3] He sees Paul as responding to specific questions in 7:1, 7:25, 8:1, and 12:1, and he bases this conclusion on the appearance of the Greek phrase *peri de*, translated "now concerning" (7:1, 25; 12:1) and "now as" (8:1). Mare suggests that 16:1 may also begin a response to a question from the Corinthians, for it too starts with "now concerning."

While the preposition *peri* ("concerning" or "as") is absent from I Corinthians 11:2, the particle *de* ("now") does appear, suggesting that the verse begins Paul's answer to another question.

Although not critical to the meaning of the passage, it would be interesting to know whether I Corinthians 11:2-16 is indeed a response to a specific question from the Corinthians concerning the use of head covering in public worship. Lowery takes the view that it is:

> The theme of personal freedom exercised without regard for the needs of others or the glory of God (which characterized the issue about eating food sacrificed to idols [8:1-11:1]) seems no less a part of this section which deals with practices affecting the assembly of the church. Here too Paul responded to the Corinthians' spirit of self-indulgence by stressing the principle of glorifying God and building up each other in the church.[4]

Whether or not I Corinthians 11:2-16 is a response to a question from the Corinthians, we should note that before addressing any of their questions Paul first con-

Introduction to I Corinthians 11:2-16

cerned himself with other matters about which he had received reliable reports (I Corinthians 1:11). The issues the Corinthians thought important included marriage, eating meat offered to idols, spiritual gifts, and perhaps giving. Without doubt these are important matters. But there were deeper problems in Corinth than these, and under the inspiration of the Holy Spirit, Paul dealt with the more vital and urgent issues first.

First, the epistle addressed the problem of envy, strife, and division in the Corinthian church (chapters 1-3). Second, Paul corrected the church for judgmental attitudes, especially toward those in leadership (chapter 4). Third, he sternly rebuked the Corinthian church for its toleration of sin (chapter 5). Fourth, he reproved the believers for going to court against their brethren and warned them against moral impurity (chapter 6).

Only after dealing with these pressing issues did Paul turn to the questions asked by the Corinthians. While nothing in the Scripture is unimportant, there is a principle of dealing first with the basic, fundamental matters. As Jesus said, some matters are weightier than others (Matthew 23:23).

The right position on eating food offered to idols would have been of little value to the Corinthians if their relationships were still torn by strife and division. The smooth operation of the spiritual gifts would have been hypocritical if the Corinthians had persisted in their judgmentalism. And being properly covered or uncovered during prayer and prophecy would have been a mockery if fornication were still tolerated in their midst.

It would be every bit as shameful for us today if we understood perfectly the doctrine of head covering but

Hair Length in the Bible

practiced favoritism, judgmentalism, and envy. It would do little good for our heads to be properly covered or uncovered if we sued a brother in a secular court, going to law with him before unbelievers (I Corinthians 6:6). The ultimate proof of discipleship is not head covering; it is whether we love one another as Christ loved us (John 13:34-35). Jesus' prayer in John 17:20-22 for unity in the church cannot be fulfilled in us if we succumb to a party spirit and are divided into numerous splinter groups. Rather than merely noting our head coverings or lack of them, sinners should note our oneness of spirit and purpose, a oneness that results in good works, which in turn give glory to God (Matthew 5:16; I Peter 2:9, 12).

When we turn to the latter part of Paul's first epistle to the believers at Corinth, it is evident that I Corinthians 11:2-14:40 addresses three major issues related to church worship. The first is submission to authority as symbolized by head covering (11:2-16). The second is the commemoration of the death of Christ by means of the Lord's Supper (11:17-34). The third is the use of spiritual gifts (12:1-14:40).

It is clear that the Corinthians were abusing the Lord's Supper and spiritual gifts. It is not so clear whether they were also in error on the matter of the covering of the head. But if they were not actually erring on this issue, they were apparently at least in danger of doing so.

William J. Martin takes the position that there is no actual rebuke in the passage:

> The first thing to note about this passage is that it is an "approving" passage ("Now I praise you" etc., v. 2), whereas the next section beginning at verse 17

Introduction to I Corinthians 11:2-16

is a "disapproving" section ("I praise you not" etc.). Any wrong or undesirable practices, therefore, referred to in the first section would be *ipso facto* only in a hypothetical sense.[5]

With these preliminary observations in mind, let us turn to an examination of I Corinthians 11:2-16.

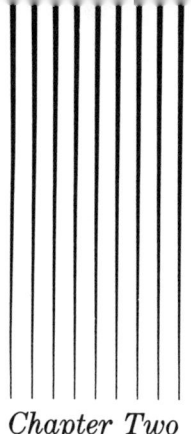

Chapter Two

Analysis of I Corinthians 11:2-16

Now I praise you, brethren, that ye remember me in all things, and keep the ordinances, as I delivered them to you (I Corinthians 11:2).

While much of the book of I Corinthians is made up of rebuke and correction, here Paul commended the Corinthian brethren for their remembrance of him and their faithfulness in keeping the ordinances he had previously communicated to them. The word *ordinances* is translated from the Greek *paradosis*, which Paul used elsewhere in both a positive and negative way, and which is more commonly translated "traditions" (Galatians 1:14; Colossians 2:8; II Thessalonians 2:15; 3:6). The internal evidence of the book suggests that these "ordinances" or traditions included teaching concerning the Lord's Supper and the gospel of the death, burial, and resurrection of Jesus Christ (I Corinthians 11:23; 15:3-4). While there were excesses and abuses in the Corinthian church, at least it had

Hair Length in the Bible

not discarded these truths.

But I would have you know, that the head of every man is Christ; and the head of the woman is the man; and the head of Christ is God (I Corinthians 11:3).

Verse 3 thus introduces the subject of the passage: headship. This important concept is expressed in the relationships between man and Christ, woman and man, and Christ and God.

The meaning of the word *head* (Greek, *kephale*) has been the subject of considerable debate. At issue is whether it refers to authority or origin. As D. A. Carson points out, the "relevant lexica are full of examples, all culled from the ancient texts, in which *kephale* connotes 'authority,' " but there is a notable paucity of data indicating a reference to "origin" or "source."[1] While Lowery agrees that the word refers primarily to authority ("subordination" is his word), he suggests that the idea of origination is also found in I Corinthians 11:8.[2] It seems that the major focus of the passage is on relationships of authority and submission, while also recognizing source or origin.

It is essential not to overlook the principle of authority when considering the passage. Proper practice in matters of head covering is meaningless unless a person understands his or her place in the economy of God. Man is directly under the headship of Christ; woman is directly under the headship of man; Christ is directly under the headship of God.

Headship and submission do not imply superiority and inferiority; the issue is responsibility and relationship. (See

Analysis of I Corinthians 11:2-16

the discussion of I Corinthians 11:11-12.) In the context, man as the head of woman is compared to Christ as the head of man and God as the head of Christ. Like any type or symbol, this one has its limits and cannot be pressed to the extreme. That is, man is not to the woman *all* that Christ is to the man. Indeed, man and woman are equal in standing before God (Galatians 3:28).

A husband is the head of his wife in the sense that he is responsible for her; he is to protect her, provide for her, and offer guidance to her. The following passages explain this truth.

For the husband is the head of the wife, even as Christ is the head of the church: and he is the saviour of the body. . . . Husbands, love your wives, even as Christ also loved the church, and gave himself for it; that he might sanctify and cleanse it with the washing of water by the word, that he might present it to himself a glorious church, not having spot, or wrinkle, or any such thing; but that it should be holy and without blemish. So ought men to love their wives as their own bodies. He that loveth his wife loveth himself. . . . For this cause shall a man leave his father and mother, and shall be joined unto his wife, and they two shall be one flesh. . . . Nevertheless let every one of you in particular so love his wife even as himself (Ephesians 5:23, 25-28, 31, 33).

Likewise, ye husbands, dwell with them according to knowledge, giving honour unto the wife, as unto the weaker vessel, and as being heirs together of the grace of life; that your prayers be not hindered (I Peter 3:7).

A wife is to allow her husband to fulfill his role, submitting to his loving, sacrificial leadership as the church submits to Christ. The following passages enunciate this principle.

Wives, submit yourselves unto your own husbands, as unto the Lord. . . . Therefore as the church is subject unto Christ, so let the wives be to their own husbands in every thing. . . . Nevertheless let . . . the wife see that she reverence her husband (Ephesians 5:22, 24, 33).

Likewise, ye wives, be in subjection to your own husbands. . . . For after this manner in the old time the holy women also, who trusted in God, adorned themselves, being in subjection unto their own husbands: even as Sara obeyed Abraham, calling him lord: whose daughters ye are, as long as ye do well, and are not afraid with any amazement (I Peter 3:1, 5-6).

The phrase "the head of Christ is God" must not be taken to mean that Christ and God are two separate persons. The main thrust of this verse and passage is not the nature of the Godhead; we must explore that truth in sections of Scripture dealing specifically with that subject. Then we can bring the understanding gained in an examination of such passages to verses like this. When we study all the Scriptures we find that there is but one God, who manifested Himself in the flesh in the person of Jesus Christ (Deuteronomy 6:4; I Timothy 3:16; Titus 2:13-14).

The word *Christ* (Greek, *christos,* "anointed one") is the Greek equivalent of the Hebrew word *Messiah*. The

Analysis of I Corinthians 11:2-16

word *Messiah* or *Christ* refers to the manifestation of God in the flesh, His humanity as indwelt by deity. (See John 1:1, 14; Galatians 4:4; I Timothy 3:16.)

The phrase "the head of Christ is God" refers to the relationship between God as an invisible, omnipresent Spirit (John 4:24) and His visible expression in human form (Philippians 2:6-9; Colossians 1:15; Hebrews 1:3). The Father (God as an invisible, omnipresent Spirit being) dwelt in Jesus Christ (a man born miraculously of a virgin) (John 14:10-11). With respect to His humanity, Jesus could say, "My Father is greater than I" (John 14:28), yet with respect to His identity as God He could say, "He that hath seen me hath seen the Father" (John 14:9).

Any attempt to make I Corinthians 11:3 refer to a separation of persons, as in trinitarianism, is faulty. If two divine persons were in view here, then the first person would have authority over the second person. The result would be a form of subordination, whereas trinitarians say that the persons are coequal.

Every man praying or prophesying, having his head covered, dishonoureth his head (I Corinthians 11:4).

At issue is a man's proper deportment while praying or while prophesying. If his head is covered at either time, he dishonors his head. The phrase "having his head covered" refers to his literal head, while the phrase "dishonoureth his head" could refer to Christ, the head of every man. The reason later given as to why a man must not have his head covered is that he is the image and glory of God (I Corinthians 11:7). If his head were

Hair Length in the Bible

covered during prayer or prophecy, he would fail to display the image and glory of God correctly. Thus, for a man to pray or prophesy with an uncovered head is a symbol of his submission to Christ's headship.

An important question here is what the phrase "having his head covered" means. Some suggest that it refers to an artificial or material covering of cloth or other substance, such as a veil or hat. Mare, for example, says, "The phrase *kata kephales echon* is to be interpreted as meaning 'having something on the head' (literally, 'having [something] down from [or over] one's head'), such as a veil."[3]

The *New International Version,* in a footnote, offers an alternate translation: "Every man who prays or prophesies with long hair dishonors his head."

Lowery does not think this meaning is probable: "The alternate translation in the NIV margin, which interprets the man's covering as long hair, is largely based on the view that verse 15 equated the covering with long hair. It is unlikely, however, that this was the point of verse 4."[4] Martin, on the other hand, is of the opinion that verse 4 does indeed refer to long hair on a man in the phrase "having his head covered." He suggests the following translation of *kata kephales echon:* "having the (hair) hanging down," and he points out that Chrysostom understood this verse to refer to long hair.[5]

It should be noted that verse 4 does not use the word *covering* as a noun. That is, the verse does not identify the covering. Martin puts *hair* in parentheses because the word does not occur in the text. But neither does any other noun appear that would specify the nature of the covering. Indeed, as Martin points out, "Nowhere in the

Analysis of I Corinthians 11:2-16

passage is any word ever used for a material veil or headdress."[6] That is, the only covering identified specifically anywhere in I Corinthians 11:2-16 is long hair (I Corinthians 11:15).

It is wrong to say that the verb *cover* means *veil*. Merle Ruth's comments provide an example of this somewhat common error:

> The word *cover*, as employed in verses 4-7, is derived from the Greek *katakalupto* and means "veil." ... The word translated *covering* in verse 15 is not *katakalupto,* as in the earlier verses, but *peribolaion.* If in God's reckoning the hair is the veiling, we could rightfully expect this statement to read thus: "Her hair is given her for a *katakalupto*" (veil).[7]

Assertions such as these reveal a lack of familiarity with the Greek language. *Katakalupto* does not mean "veil." It is formed from *kata,* a preposition meaning "down from" or "down upon," and *kalupto,* a verb meaning "to cover, hide, or conceal." The Greek text of verses 4-7 teaches that a man's head is to be uncovered and a woman's head is to be covered; it does not say what the covering is. Moreover, *katakalupto* in verse 6 is a verb, while *peribolaion* in verse 15 is a noun. They cannot be interchanged.

The Greek text of I Corinthians 11:2-16 does not specifically speak of a material headdress. While it is possible that propriety in Corinth at the time demanded that modest women wear a veil, the text avoids using any word that would demand garment veils on Christian women of all eras or forbid men to wear hats or other material cover-

Hair Length in the Bible

ings while praying or prophesying.
The phrase "having his head covered" is *kata kephales echon* in Greek. *Kata* is a preposition meaning "down upon" or "down from," *kephales* means "head," and *echon* means "having." The literal meaning of the Greek phrase is "having [something] down upon or down from the head." Thus the KJV translation "having his head covered" is a literal rendering, and it leaves open the question of the nature of the covering.

We should note that verse 4 implies that it is physically possible for a man to pray or prophesy with his head covered. His head being covered does not necessarily invalidate his prayer or prophecy, but it does fail to properly honor (indeed, it dishonors) his authority, who is Christ.

But every woman that prayeth or prophesieth with her head uncovered dishonoureth her head: for that is even all one as if she were shaven (I Corinthians 11:5).

Just as men are to pray or prophesy with an uncovered head, so women are to do so with a covered head. In the phrase "with her head uncovered," the word *head* doubtless refers to a woman's literal head, while in the phrase "dishonoureth her head" it probably refers to her authority—her husband or father. (See verse 3.)

Like verse 4, verse 5 does not mean that it is *impossible* for a woman to pray or prophesy with an uncovered head. To the contrary, it implies that it is physically possible for her to do so. Her head being uncovered does not prohibit her from praying or prophesying, nor does it invalidate the content of the prayer or prophecy itself, but

Analysis of I Corinthians 11:2-16

it does dishonor her head, her husband or father.

Martin sees all of I Corinthians 11 as relating to the subject of headship:

> [The passage seeks] to explain the respective roles of the man and the woman *en ecclesia*, that is, in a church worship-meeting convened for the specific purpose of commemorating the Lord's Supper. . . . Man is to appear with uncovered head for he is the glorious image of God (v. 7), whom he represents and in a sense personates in the worship of the true Head. The woman, on the other hand, acts the part of the church. . . . As the man's uncovered head betokens the supremacy of the true Head, whom he represents, so it is necessary for the woman as the symbol of the church to acknowledge by her "covered" head the headship of Christ.[8]

Like verse 4, verse 5 does not specify the nature of the covering. Some commentators suggest that decorum and modesty in Corinth at that time required virtuous women to wear veils. For example, *The Pulpit Commentary* suggests that for a woman to appear in a public assembly with her head uncovered would violate custom:

> [It] was against the national custom of all ancient communities, and might lead to the gravest misconceptions. As a rule, modest women covered their heads with the *peplum* or with a veil when they worshipped or were in public. . . . If a woman appeared in public unveiled, she was deemed immodest. To wear a veil was a sign of womanly delicacy. . . . If she went

to a public assembly without her veil, she acted shamelessly. To be consistent, argues St. Paul, "let her also be shorn," and so assume the mark of a disreputable woman. A woman acting in this way sets public opinion at defiance; and as public opinion in many things is public conscience . . . no woman could do this thing and not shock all right sensibility. Besides, the veil is a sign of subordination and dependence. Refusing to use this covering of the head was a mark of insubordination and independence. A symbol it was, but to cast off the symbol was to repudiate the thing signified.[9]

Others have variously suggested that public prostitutes advertised their availability by appearing in public unveiled, that women convicted of immorality were shaven and sentenced to a public, bareheaded display of guilt, and that heathen priestesses "prophesied" unveiled, with disheveled hair.

Lowery states that it was the custom for women to wear a head covering in public:

> It cannot be unequivocally asserted but the preponderance of evidence points toward the public head covering of women as a universal custom in the first century in both Jewish culture . . . and Greco-Roman culture. . . . The nature of the covering varied considerably . . . but it was commonly a portion of the outer garment drawn up over the head like a hood.[10]

In light of this custom, Bruce K. Waltke concludes that verses 5-6 refer to a material head covering: "It

Analysis of I Corinthians 11:2-16

seems probable to suppose that some of the individualistic Corinthians were proposing that their women throw off their traditional veils which symbolized their subordination to the men."[11] He quotes Morna Hooker, a professor of divinity at Cambridge University: "According to Jewish custom a bride went bareheaded until her marriage, as a symbol of her freedom; when married, she wore a veil as a sign that she was under the authority of her husband."[12]

It should be noted, however, that Paul does not address husbands and wives in I Corinthians 11; he addresses men and women. Thus an unmarried Jewish girl who followed Jewish custom by remaining bareheaded would dishonor her head if she, as a Christian convert, prayed or prophesied. Moreover, the Talmud, which may preserve teaching from this time, tells Jewish males to wear a skull cap when praying. But it is doubtful that Jewish custom, whatever it may have been, had any bearing on the situation among the Christians at Corinth.

Waltke quotes Jeremias as he describes the veil of a Jewish woman: "Her face was hidden by an arrangement of two head veils, a headband on the forehead with bands on the chin, and a hairnet with ribbons and knots, so that her features could not be recognized."[13] Though Waltke concludes, "It would be well for Christian women to wear head coverings at church meetings as a symbol of an abiding theological truth," he does not suggest that such head coverings fit the description given by Jeremias![14]

Not all commentators agree that verses 5-6 refer to a garment veil. William J. Martin makes a strong case that they refer to long hair:

Hair Length in the Bible

> Several indications show beyond reasonable doubt that Paul is using the term "covered" to refer to long hair. First, he uses it in contradistinction to the state of the man who is debarred from "having the (hair) hanging down" (verse 4). To make the wearing of a head-covering the opposite of short hair would be a false antithesis. It would have been pharisaical casuistry and sheer quibbling to say that wearing a head-covering compensated for being shorn. To annul the state of being shorn you must be the opposite. To be transparently honest Paul would have had to say there is only one way, one simple, plain, unambiguous, right way to efface the shame of being shorn and that is to have long hair; and that is surely what Paul is saying. Second, nowhere in the passage is any word ever used for a material veil or head-dress. Third, as the forms of the verb *katakalupto* [to cover] found here [verses 6-7] are not construed with an indirect object, it is best to take them as passive. Fourth, in v. 15 Paul states unequivocally that a woman's long hair takes the place of an item of dress. Besides, one would expect Paul to use some more explicit term for "unveiled."[15]

We have previously considered Martin's first and second points. His third point is that the verb *katakalupto* in verses 6-7 has no indirect object and that it is therefore better to understand it as passive. In other words, it does not speak of something that covers the woman but of the fact that she is covered.

Verses 5-6 do not say a woman must "put on a covering," they simply indicate that she must be "covered."

Analysis of I Corinthians 11:2-16

If she has her natural covering of hair (verse 15), she apparently does not need to put anything else on her head; she is "covered." If she does not have her natural covering of hair, she can cover her head with an artificial covering if she wishes, but she is still in shame, for it is a shame for her to have her hair cut (verse 6).

Verse 5 points out that for the woman to pray or prophesy with her head uncovered is equivalent to her being shaven. There is no question about what "shaven" means. A woman whose head has been shaven has received an obvious mark of shame. According to Deuteronomy 21:10-14, God considers the shaving of a woman's head to be a humiliation to her.

For if the woman be not covered, let her also be shorn: but if it be a shame for a woman to be shorn or shaven, let her be covered (I Corinthians 11:6).

It is possible to interpret this verse in at least two ways. One interpretation is that if a woman is not covered (whatever that word means), then she should theoretically be shorn. In other words, it is no more a shame for her to be shorn than to be uncovered.

This view seems to imply that the covering is a material veil that a woman should wear in addition to her uncut hair. Otherwise, the phrase "For if the woman be not covered, let her also be shorn" is difficult to understand. If long, uncut hair is her covering, she is automatically shorn when she cuts it and to be uncovered and to be shorn are identical states. But the word *also* seems to imply that the shearing of her hair is something done because she is not covered.

Hair Length in the Bible

The latter part of the verse reveals that it is equally a shame for a woman to be shorn or shaven. The word *shorn* is the past participle of the verb *shear*. It is translated from the Greek *keiro,* which means "to have one's hair cut" without specifying how much is cut off.[16] We should carefully note this fact: both the Greek *keiro* and the English *shear* simply refer to cutting. The word does not specify how much hair is cut off or how much is left after the cutting. The hair is shorn if any of it is cut off. For this reason, several translations render *keiro* as "cut off" or "cut" instead of "shorn."[17]

Thus, if a woman is not covered, it is the moral equivalent of her being shorn, of having her hair cut. Since it is a shame for a woman to be shorn (to have her hair cut) or shaved (to have her hair shaved off), she should be covered.

Martin explains the shame associated with the cutting of a woman's hair:

> There was evidently something undesirable and even disreputable associated with shorn hair.... Shorn hair among the Jews was a sign of mourning (Job 1:20; Jer. 7:29; Mic. 1:16). The use of the definite article in *he exuremene* "the shorn woman" (v. 5) would seem to point to the existence of a specific class to whom this designation could be applied. Paul in any case would have disapproved of the practice because of its association with heathen superstition. The practice of cutting off the hair among the Greeks as a religious rite is well attested. The Vestal virgins and all Greek girls did it on reaching puberty. The earliest form of the custom appears to have been the vow or dedica-

tion of hair to a river, to be fulfilled at puberty or at some crisis, or after deliverance from danger. Some of the Hellenized Jewesses may well have copied their Greek neighbours.[18]

The word *shame* is translated from the Greek *aischron,* which Paul used four times. (See also I Corinthians 14:35; Ephesians 5:12; Titus 1:11.) It refers to something that is shameful, disgraceful, or even dishonest.

To summarize, one interpretation of verse 6 is that a woman is to be covered with a veil; if she is not, she may as well, for all practical purposes, be shorn. Since, however, it is a shame for a woman to be shorn or shaven, she should also wear the veil.

A second interpretation is that verse 6 speaks only of long hair as the head covering for a woman. This view is represented by William Martin and a footnote in the New International Version.

Following his line of thinking that the covering throughout the passage is long hair, Martin offers the following translation of verse 6:

For if a woman is not covered (has not long hair) then let her remain cropped (for the time being; *keirastho,* aorist imperative with cessative force, referring to a particular situation), but since it is a shame for a woman to be cropped or shorn let her become covered—(i.e. let her hair grow again; *katakaluptestho,* present imperative for non-terminative, inchoative action).[19]

Martin justifies his translation as follows:

Hair Length in the Bible

It would be unthinkable that among Paul's many converts there were not women of the "shorn woman" class. What then was to be done about their inability to conform with the requirement of having long hair? Were they to be excluded until such time as nature would remedy their lack? Certainly not. It would have been monstrous to exclude any believer from the immediate enjoyment of the privileges of church fellowship.[20]

Martin's position on verse 6 is supported by the alternate translation offered by a footnote in the *New International Version:* "If a woman has no covering, let her be for now with short hair, but since it is a disgrace for a woman to have her hair shorn or shaved, she should grow it again." It must be recognized, however, that this translation is not strictly literal; it is a paraphrase. The Greek has no noun for "covering," nor does it mention "hair" in verse six. The NIV's footnote is actually a commentary on the verse.

Is it possible, though, that verse 6 should be understood in this way? Does it address the problem of new converts who come into the assembly with cut hair, saying they can enter the full privileges of fellowship even though their hair is shorn, while overcoming this shame by growing their hair?

The question seems to hinge on the use of the word *also.* In modern English, the word means "in addition to" or "too." Thus the verse seems to mean, "For if the woman be not covered, let her in addition be shorn." If this interpretation is correct, then the covering of verse 6 is not long hair, for if she had removed this covering

Analysis of I Corinthians 11:2-16

by cutting her hair, she would already be shorn. Being shorn would not be something in addition to being covered.

This understanding of *also* is the strongest point in favor of those who insist that the verse 6 refers to a second covering of a garment veil or headdress. While there is no Greek word or English word (in the KJV) for "covering" (other than the designation of long hair as a covering in verse 15), the word *also* in verse 6 seems to imply a covering in addition to long hair.

If, however, the word *also* in verse 6 does not mean "in addition to," the verse would permit the meaning suggested by Martin and the NIV footnote. The word *also* is translated from the Greek *kai,* which is a simple conjunction meaning "and," "even," or "also." The meaning of "even" would fit well with this second interpretation of verse 6.

It is interesting to note that at the time of the King James translation in 1611, the English word *also* had a similar range of meaning. The word originally came from two words, *all* and *so*. In Middle English, the word *all* meant "wholly" or "quite." Thus, *also* meant "wholly so" or "quite so."

In conclusion, it is possible that we should understand verse 6 as follows: if a woman is presently uncovered because she has cut her hair, she should be permitted ("let," KJV) even to be in that condition (of being shorn) while enjoying the fellowship of the church. But since it is a shame for her to be in that condition (of being shorn or shaven), she should allow her hair to grow again.

We should note that neither of these two interpretations of verse 6 negates the teaching of verse 15 that a woman is to have long, uncut hair. The only debatable issue is whether the Corinthian women had to wear a second covering of a veil and whether such a requirement applies to Christian women today.

For the sake of discussion, let us suppose that verses 5-6 did indeed teach the Corinthian women to wear a material headdress. Must Christian women of all ages follow this practice? We do not believe so, for the following reasons.

1. *If the veiling of women was a custom in Corinth, it was only a temporary, localized custom.* If Paul taught the women there to wear veils, he did so only because it was expected of proper women in that culture, not because going without a veil would be inherently immoral, immodest, or vain.

The veiling of women has not been practiced uniformly from ancient history, nor has it been widely practiced during the past many centuries. While a Christian woman should do nothing to identify herself with immorality, regardless of the culture in which she lives, some practices are neutral in themselves and vary in meaning from culture to culture and generation to generation.

Paul was concerned with the identification of the Christian woman at Corinth with immoral or heathen women. While the Bible deals with cultural issues current to its writing, it does not attempt to anticipate every culture to come. Rather, it reveals principles by which Christians in any culture can direct their lives.

As the following quotations from reference works show, the wearing of veils has not been practiced consistently from ancient times.

Analysis of I Corinthians 11:2-16

There is relatively little material on veils worn by women in the Old Testament. The Talmud has no designation for "veil." The veiled ladies of the present-day Muslim communities would have been out of place, for the most part, in Old Testament times. It follows that several of the terms rendered "veil" in the Bible do not really refer to veils but to ornamental coverings of one kind or another, and their specific meanings are far from clear.[21]

In Genesis 38, one motive for Tamar's use of the veil was certainly to avoid recognition, but it seems clear from the passage that veils were used by courtesans [prostitutes]. . . . The use of the face veil as a regular article of dress was unknown to Hebrew women. . . . The modern oriental custom of veiling is due to Mohammedan influence and has not been universally adopted by Jewesses in the Orient. In New Testament times, however, among both Greeks and Romans, reputable women wore a veil in public and to appear without it was an act of bravado. Tarsus, Paul's home city, was especially noted for strictness in this regard. Hence Paul's indignant directions in I Corinthians 11:2-16, which have their basis in the social proprieties of the time.[22]

The use of the veil by the bride (Genesis 24:65) and in other cases (Genesis 38:14; Ruth 3:3) is traceable to the influence of the Ishtar myth. The veil was the symbol of Ishtar, who on coming from the underworld, walked out veiled to meet Tammuz, her bridegroom. Otherwise, it was not customary for women to go veiled and according to Genesis 12:14; 24:15 contrary to present custom in the Orient due to the influence of Islam. As regarding headdresses, some representations show Jews and Syrians bareheaded, others show them wearing a band to hold the hair together.[23]

Clearly, it is difficult to prove from history that the wearing of veils has been customary in all ages by godly women. In fact, the preceding references suggest that the wearing of veils has often been connected with an undesirable history. They were used by prostitutes, were connected to the pagan Ishtar myth, and presently owe their use among Oriental women to the influence of Islam.

2. *The original plan of God does not indicate that women were to wear head veils.*

Jesus appealed to the original plan of God when the Pharisees questioned Him about divorce in Matthew 19. Jesus responded by teaching them how it was at the beginning. The Pharisees appealed to culture and custom that had developed during the intervening years since the beginning. They protested, "Why did Moses then command to give a writing of divorcement, and to put her away?" (Matthew 19:7). The Lord replied, "Moses because of the hardness of your hearts suffered you to put away your wives: but from the beginning it was not so" (Matthew 19:8).

Moses, a civil as well as religious leader, was forced to make some kind of judgment to deal with the sinfulness of the Israelites. He had a choice of allowing them to practice unrestrained hedonism, with no rules and regulations, or he could make the best of a bad situation. He chose

Analysis of I Corinthians 11:2-16

the latter, insisting that if there were to be divorce, it was to be done in a consistent, recordable way. This is not to say it was God's will for the Israelites to practice divorce for every cause; it was not. Jesus refused to be drawn into this argument; He bypassed the customs that had developed during the ensuing years and were based on human sinfulness, and He went back to the very beginning for the correct teaching.

The same principle reveals that Christian women are not required to wear veils today. From the beginning it was not so. When God created Adam and Eve, He did not instruct Eve to wear an artificial veil. He did not provide her with such a covering. Instead, He provided her with a natural covering of hair. Nothing additional was required for her to be present when the voice of the Lord walked in the garden in the cool of the day. Even after Adam and Eve's sin and expulsion from the Garden of Eden, we read nothing of God commanding Eve to veil herself when approaching Him. There is not even a hint that He required such a thing. Surely, if God desired women to be veiled, He would have said so. Instead, He provided women with a natural veil.

3. *Long, uncut hair is given to a woman instead of a veil.*

This point will be discussed more completely with I Corinthians 11:15. But for now we should note that the word *for* in the phrase "her hair is given her for a covering" is translated from the Greek *anti*, a word which means "against" or "instead of." This is the meaning of the word according to Dana and Mantey's *Grammar*, Bauer's *Lexicon*, Thayer's *Lexicon*, and Gingrich's *Shorter Lexicon of the Greek New Testament*. Several translations render the word "instead of" in this verse. Of course, the English word *for* can also mean "instead of."

In summary, no passage of Scripture clearly commands a woman to wear a material headdress; it is not certain that this passage refers to such a covering; even if it does, it reflects a temporary, localized practice; the wearing of veils seems to be of questionable origin; veils do not appear as part of God's plan in the beginning; and this passage declares that a woman's long hair is her covering. All these points indicate that Christian women in this era need not wear a material headdress. On the other hand, if a Christian woman were part of a culture where a veil symbolized modesty and her lack of compliance would place her in disrepute, she should adhere to the local custom.

For a man indeed ought not to cover his head, forasmuch as he is the image and glory of God: but the woman is the glory of the man (I Corinthians 11:7).

The reason why a man ought not to cover his head is that he is the image and glory of God. It seems that if a man's head were covered he would not properly symbolize the headship of Christ. It is perhaps not necessary to understand *why* God ordained that this is so; it is enough to know that He did. Not only should men fulfill the symbol, but they should conduct themselves in such a way as to reflect the image of God and bring glory to Him.

As far as the symbolism of this passage is concerned, the woman, while also created in the image of God, is the glory of the man. "A virtuous woman is a crown to her

Analysis of I Corinthians 11:2-16

husband" (Proverbs 12:4). A crown is a symbol of authority and majesty, or glory. While a man's covered head detracts from the headship of Christ, a woman's uncovered head detracts from the headship of her husband or father. We must remember that the covering or lack of it is a symbol only, but that to cast away the symbol is to repudiate in the eyes of God the thing symbolized.

We must not think that the symbolism is important only during prayer or prophecy. Since man is the image and glory of God and woman is the glory of man at all times, not just during spiritual exercises, it is important for the man's head to be uncovered and the woman's head to be covered at all times. While verses 4-5 address prayer and prophecy, verses 6-15 seem to depart from that limited frame of reference. Verses 14-15 are especially clear in this regard.

Why then does the passage mention restrictions with reference to prayer and prophecy? It could be that the Corinthians advanced this specific question. Or Paul could have chosen to argue from the obvious specific case to the more general case. If the Corinthians saw the proper deportment for prayer and prophecy, then they could more easily understand the reasonableness of this position as it pertained to all of life.

If indeed this passage applies to all of life and not just to prayer and prophecy, it would strongly indicate that material headdresses are not in view. Few would forbid a man to wear a hat or other covering at all times, and few would insist that a woman wear a veil every moment of the day.

Moreover, it would be strange indeed if a garment woven by hand were actually instrumental in influencing

Hair Length in the Bible

or preventing a virtuous woman's approach to God, especially when the church has immediate access to God through the blood of Jesus Christ and men and women have equal spiritual standing (Hebrews 10:19-20; Galatians 3:28). New Testament circumcision is not made by hands (Colossians 2:11-12), and spiritual life under the new covenant is not based on ceremonial law (Colossians 2:16-17). Thus it is difficult to imagine a headdress playing a role in spirituality. This idea seems akin to the Pharisaic emphasis on long garments and broad phylacteries (Matthew 23:5). By contrast, long hair is a natural covering given by God, and He has invested it with a significance that we are to observe and maintain.

If a material headdress were required by God in order for a woman to pray or prophesy, it would be serious business indeed, and it would be important to have the right headdress precisely. But Scripture offers no clue as to the style or length of such a piece of clothing. It would certainly seem that many modern interpretations of a material headdress—hats, minute bonnets, and small squares of lace—would fall far short of a covering that "hangs down" and is "thrown about" a person's head. The only thing that certainly and surely fulfills this description is the long hair of verses 14-15.

For the man is not of the woman; but the woman of the man. Neither was the man created for the woman; but the woman for the man (I Corinthians 11:8-9).

The rationale of these verses reaches back into the dawn of human history at creation. God has decreed this symbolism because of the order at creation and the distinc-

Analysis of I Corinthians 11:2-16

tion of the sexes. Man was created first; then the woman was made from a rib in his side. Since the woman was not made first, man was not created for her; she was created for him, to complete him (Genesis 2:18). Their roles are complementary but distinct.

While God gave the man and the woman certain unchangeable physical characteristics to distinguish them, He allowed them to possess one changeable distinguishing characteristic. They could manipulate the hair. That is, a man can allow his hair to grow and a woman can cut hers if they wish. By conforming instead to God's standard, they demonstrate their willingness to accept the role God has given them and to fulfill His purposes for their lives. The unchangeable physical characteristics are God's part; the changeable one is theirs.

For this cause ought the woman to have power on her head because of the angels (I Corinthians 11:10).

This verse has given rise to many interpretations. First, there is a debate as to whether it speaks of evil, fallen angels or the angels of God. Then there is the question of what the phrase "power on her head" means.

The angels spoken of could be all angels, fallen and faithful, for both groups are very aware of the activities of individuals. The fallen angels observe human events for opportunities to destroy. The faithful angels do the same to protect, guide, strengthen, and minister to the children of God (Hebrews 1:14). A woman who submits to her authority and who displays that submission by her long hair enjoys protection from evil spirits bent on her destruction and also enjoys the benefits that accrue to

Hair Length in the Bible

the people of God. In this way her long hair is "power" on her head, power against evil and for good.

A rebellious woman does not have this power. (See I Samuel 15:23.) And a woman who is submissive in spirit but who through ignorance lacks the outward sign of that submission at the least confuses matters in the spirit realm.

Nevertheless neither is the man without the woman, neither the woman without the man, in the Lord. For as the woman is of the man, even so is the man also by the woman; but all things of God (I Corinthians 11:11-12).

These verses now point out that man and woman are on equal footing in the sight of God. (See also Galatians 3:28.) It seems that this teaching is inserted in the midst of the passage to prevent anyone from falsely concluding that man is superior to woman. The subject of the passage is not superiority and inferiority, but responsibility and authority.

While woman originally came from man, every man after Adam has come from a woman. Because their roles are complementary and not equivalent, they are equally important to each other, to families, to society, and to the church. Man and woman are equal in worth, intellect, human rights, and spiritual matters, but their roles and relationships—which the head covering symbolizes—are different. In the final analysis, both man and woman come from God and derive their value and uniqueness from Him.

Judge in yourselves: is it comely that a woman pray

Analysis of I Corinthians 11:2-16

unto God uncovered? Doth not even nature itself teach you, that, if a man have long hair, it is a shame unto him? But if a woman have long hair, it is a glory to her: for her hair is given her for a covering (I Corinthians 11:13-15).

Paul thought the Corinthians capable of judging the appropriateness of women praying uncovered. Upon what basis would they be able to make this judgment? The basis was nature, or instinct, which has, by and large, caused all societies at all times to recognize the inappropriateness of men having long hair and the appropriateness of women having long hair. While people have violated this principle at various times and places, the fact remains: on a man, long hair is considered uncomely; on a woman, it is thought beautiful. Why is this? It is because of the inbred sense of propriety that has been in humanity from the beginning.

A question generally arises at this point: How long must one's hair be to fit the biblical definition of "long"? The answer centers on the meaning of the Greek words *koma* (a verb) and *kome* (a noun).

Koma is translated "have long hair" both in verses 14 and 15. According to Gingrich's lexicon, the word means to "wear long hair, let one's hair grow long." Thayer's lexicon renders it "to let the hair grow, have long hair." Obviously, someone cannot allow hair to grow and cut it at the same time.

Kome is the word translated "hair" in the phrase "for her hair is given her for a covering" (verse 15). The passages cited by Bauer's lexicon and Moulton and Miligan's *Vocabulary of the Greek New Testament* indicate that *kome* refers to uncut hair. The passages cited by these

Hair Length in the Bible

works in which this word occurs in Greek literature demand the meaning of "uncut hair." The word *kome* is also used to describe the Nazarites, who were forbidden to cut their hair.[24]

Long hair is hair that has not been shorn, or cut; it has been allowed to grow. It does not require a specific length, or it would be necessary for the Scripture to specify that length to insure conformity. Such an artificial measurement would exclude some women from the privilege of ever having long hair, since due to physical and hereditary factors the length of women's uncut hair varies greatly. The only way all women could be assured of fulfilling the admonition to be covered with long hair is if the definition of long is uncut.

The statement "for her hair is given her for a covering" is critical to the entire passage, for it provides the only specific definition of a covering in the passage. (See the discussion of verse 6.)

The word *for* is translated from the Greek *anti*, which means "against" or "instead of." Webster's dictionary offers thirty-one definitions for the preposition *for*. The first is "against; in the place of; as a substitute or equivalent . . . like the Gr[eek] *anti*." The second definition is "in the place of; instead of; noting substitution of persons, or agency of one in the place of another with equivalent authority." The third definition is "in exchange of; noting one thing taken or given in place of another."[25]

A woman's long, uncut hair is given to her for, or instead of, a covering. Her hair, when she allows it to grow without cutting it, serves as her covering. A woman's long hair is the only actual covering mentioned in the entire passage.

Analysis of I Corinthians 11:2-16

What does the phrase "If a man have long hair, it is a shame unto him" mean? The Greek word translated "long hair" here is the same one earlier translated "long hair" in reference to women. The point is that if a man allows his hair to grow uncut, it is widely recognized to be shameful.

This is not to suggest that a man does well if he merely cuts his hair with great infrequency. Underlying this entire passage is the Bible teaching of the distinction between men and women. While a man might be able to escape the technical definition of "long hair" by having his hair cut once in a great while, he could very well violate the spirit of the passage by giving the appearance of having uncut hair and by blurring the distinction between the sexes. The woman's hair should be clearly long and uncut; the man's hair should be clearly short and cut. While the accepted length of men's hair may vary slightly from culture to culture and time to time, by and large all societies have recognized the propriety of man having hair so short that it is clearly cut and uniquely masculine.

But if any man seem to be contentious, we have no such custom, neither the churches of God (I Corinthians 11:16).

There seem to be three basic interpretations of this verse.

First, some claim Paul essentially said, "I have told you what I believe. However, if you don't agree with it, do as you please." Some would go further to suppose that Paul said, "Neither we nor the churches of God have any custom of women being covered when they pray or prophesy."

It is unreasonable, however, to suppose that Paul

would take the time and space he did in I Corinthians 11:2-15 to teach on important matters relating to prayer and prophecy, only to throw it all away if his readers disagreed. If everyone should do what was right in his own eyes on this issue, surely Paul would have said so at the beginning, rather than carefully stating the proper view and supporting it with the teaching of nature. Moreover, why would God inspire Paul to write this passage and then, in effect, cancel it?

If this interpretation of verse 16 were correct, I Corinthians 11 would probably have read something like this: "Now I praise you, brethren, that ye remember me in all things, and keep the ordinances, as I delivered them unto you. But I would have you know that every man should make up his own mind as to whether a man ought to uncover his head when he prays or prophesies and whether a woman ought to cover hers when doing the same." Then it would have proceeded to discuss the Lord's Supper. Instead, Paul carefully dealt with the issue, and it is unreasonable to think he would casually and flippantly toss away all he had just said with the equivalent of "It really doesn't matter."

We must realize that contention is not of God. "Only by pride cometh contention: but with the well advised is wisdom" (Proverbs 13:10). If pride is the source of contention, those who would have been contentious against the inspired teaching of Paul would have been proud. Paul surely did not give these people a license to reject the will of God because they rebelled out of pride.

The second view of verse 16 is that it stands alone in the chapter, introducing and completing a discussion on a third subject: contention. In other words, those who

Analysis of I Corinthians 11:2-16

hold this view suppose that this verse simply says, "We do not have the custom of being contentious," and see it as unrelated to the verses before or after. This interpretation is strained, as it appears that verse 16 is the natural summation of the previous several verses. There seems to be no point in separating the verse from the material that has gone before, nor does there seem to be any connection between it and what comes after. Paul knew the temperament of the Corinthian church. (See I Corinthians 1:10; 3:3.) He knew some would be contentious and would wish to reject his instruction, so he anticipated their objection. And, of course, God inspired his words.

The third view, which we believe to be correct, is this: Paul, knowing some would be contentious and want to reject his teaching, anticipated their response by saying, "We have no such custom—no custom encouraging women to pray or prophesy uncovered—neither do the churches of God." Many Bible translations render the verse along this line. For example, the New International Version translates verse 16, "If anyone wants to be contentious about this, we have no other practice—nor do the churches of God." And *The Pulpit Commentary* explains, "Paul cuts the question short, as though impatient of any further discussion of a subject already settled by instinctive decorum and by the common sense of universal usage."[26] In this way, verse 16 concludes the teaching on this subject.

In summary, I Corinthians 11:2-16 teaches that it is a shame for a woman to be shorn, shaven, or to pray or prophesy with her head uncovered and that it is a shame for a man to pray or prophesy with his head covered. Paul

Hair Length in the Bible

appealed to the common knowledge of the time that a woman should be covered with the long hair God has provided her while a man should not have long hair. Then he assured his readers that anyone who was contentious on this issue would be in opposition to his practice and to that of the churches of God in general.

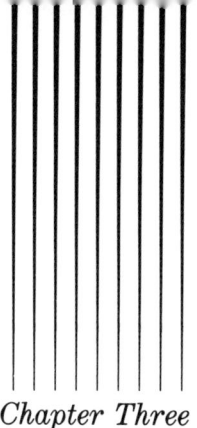

Chapter Three

The Voice of History

Nowhere does Scripture speak favorably of women cutting their hair. The Bible does not have a great deal to say on this subject, probably because the proper view has been so readily accepted throughout history, having been an instinctive lesson of nature. *The New Schaff-Herzog Encyclopedia of Religious Knowledge* explains the situation in biblical times:

> Women never cut their hair (cf. Jer. vii. 29), and long hair was their greatest ornament (Cant. iv. 1; cf. I Cor. xi. 15; Cant. vii. 5). To cut off a woman's hair and so expose her neck was the greatest contumely [humiliation] (cf. Jer. vii. 29; I Cor. xi. 6).[1]

We should note how emphatic this statement is: "Women never cut their hair." The Bible similarly indicates that women wore their hair long. There are no examples in Scripture of godly women who made a prac-

Hair Length in the Bible

tice of cutting their hair.

Jeremiah cried, "Cut off thine hair, O Jerusalem, and cast it away, and take up a lamentation on high places; for the LORD hath rejected and forsaken the generation of his wrath" (Jeremiah 7:29). This verse speaks in sorrowful tones of the evil the people of Judah had done in the sight of God and of His determination to chastise them. Judah is pictured as a woman, and the height of shame for her symbolically would be to cut off her hair.

Solomon compared the beauty of long, flowing hair to "a flock of goats, that appear from mount Gilead" (Song of Solomon 4:1). This is a poetic, picturesque description. We can imagine a flock streaming over the horizon, coming in a seemingly endless parade. Our harried society may prevent some from seeing the aesthetic beauty that would have been so obvious to the Hebrew eye.

Another description of a woman's long hair is found in Song of Solomon 7:5: "Thine head upon thee is like Carmel, and the hair of thine head like purple; the king is held in the galleries." This verse compares the lady's hair to the garments of purple worn by royalty.

In biblical times, one of a woman's greatest humiliations was to have her hair cut. What has happened to change the way society views the cutting of women's hair? Perhaps we can identify some general trends.

For thousands of years, society frowned upon the cutting of hair by women. In broad terms, it is only since the turn of the twentieth century that the practice has gained and held wide acceptance. One hundred years ago, to insist that a woman's hair was her glory would not have been thought strange anywhere in Christendom, regard-

The Voice of History

less of a person's denominational affiliation or lack of it. Today, however, the picture has changed. The *World Book Encyclopedia* explains when American women started cutting their hair: "Short hair styles became popular in the 1920's. Irene Castle, a famous ballroom dancer, started a fashion of bobbed [cut] hair for women."[2]

The so-called women's liberation movement today seeks to obliterate all distinctions between men and women in order to make women "equal" with men. Leaders in this movement recognize that feminine modes of behavior and appearance serve to distinguish women from men. As a result, many of them, such as Susan Brownmiller in her book *Femininity* have argued that these feminine distinctives need to be abandoned. And one significant distinctive that modern society has abandoned is long, uncut hair for women and short hair for men.

But attempts to establish equality by contradicting the Bible are misguided. In truth, only in Christ Jesus is there absolute freedom and equality for male and female (Galatians 3:28). God is no respecter of persons (Acts 10:34).

Each person has his or her proper place in the body of Christ (I Corinthians 12:27). Likewise, the male and female each have their proper, God-given roles to fulfill in life. As much as some resist the idea, God created man and woman with different functions, responsibilities, and purposes. Neither of them is inferior to the other. Both stand before God on equal footing. But rebellion against the will of God will result in a bitter harvest.

In communist nations, women are supposedly free.

Hair Length in the Bible

They claim to have already reached the goal toward which many Western women are striving. But how does it work for them? The women are "free" to work side by side with men, wielding heavy shovels and equipment. They are not free to stay home with their children but place them in state-operated child-care centers as quickly as they are weaned, so they can return to the work force. They are "free" from the duty of teaching their children religious principles, since it is a crime to do so.

While this "freedom" is already a reality in much of the communist world, there is also a strong anti-Christian "liberation" movement in democratic countries as well. For example, the *Humanist Manifesto II*—one of the signers of which was Betty Friedan, founder of the National Organization for Women—repudiates belief in God:

> We find insufficient evidence for belief in the existence of a supernatural. As non-theists, we begin with humans, not God, nature not deity. . . . But we can discover no divine purpose or providence for the human species. . . . No deity will save us; we must save ourselves. Promises of immortal salvation or fear of eternal damnation are both illusory and harmful.[3]

Gloria Steinem, editor of *Ms.* magazine, and a prominent member of the National Organization of Women, similarly stated, "By the year 2000 we will, I hope, raise our children to believe in human potential, not God."[4]

The Document, another declaration of feminism, contains this chilling renunciation of marriage:

> All of history must be rewritten in terms of the oppression of women. We must go back to ancient female

The Voice of History

religions. . . . Marriage has existed for the benefit of men and has been a legally sanctioned method of control over women. . . . The end of the institution of marriage is a necessary condition for the liberation of women. Therefore, it is important for us to encourage women to leave their husbands and not to live individually with men. . . . Now we know it is the institution that has failed us and we must work to destroy it.[5]

Dr. Mary Jo Bane, associate director of Wellesley College's Center for Research on Women and assistant professor of education, has similarly attacked the biblical institution of the family: "We really don't know how to raise children. . . . We must take them away from families and communally raise them. . . . It [divorce] makes for better family. . . . Divorce improves the quality of marriage."[6]

Statements such as these demonstrate that in many ways Western society is not improving with regard to women's role, but rather it is rapidly reaching a low of spiritual poverty.

Historically, the "liberation" of women from biblical beliefs, principles, and roles is connected with women cutting their hair. The practice did not originate with spiritual revival, but with the flapper era of the twenties. It was not godly women who decided that cutting their hair should now be acceptable, after centuries of being a disgrace. Instead, the practice of women cutting their hair was born out of the desire of women to "break the chains" of responsibility to husbands and fathers. It was not introduced to our society by a preacher, but by a dancer. The

Hair Length in the Bible

idea was at first revolting even to women who daringly embraced it. These are numerous reports that women fainted away in barber shops after seeing the results of having their hair cut. The following stories from the 1920s may be amusing or shocking today, but they illustrate vividly that the idea of a woman cutting her hair was revolutionary.

Peoria, Ill., Sept. 27. Fearing his temper would get away with him because his wife had had her hair bobbed, John Baer, 60, called at the county jail last night, begging to be locked up so he could "cool off."[7]

A petition was circulated at Warsaw and signed by thousands of orthodox Jews, asking rabbis to refuse to perform marriage ceremonies for women who have bobbed hair, wear short dresses or use rouge. The petition submitted to the rabbinical council asked that the fathers and husbands of such women be excluded from the synagogues.[8]

The army of maid servants in Buckingham Palace, England, must have long hair, or be growing it back in case they have had it bobbed. Such was the order of King George. Those not willing to wear long hair must give up their royal jobs.[9]

The women of the municipality of Wartenburg, East Prussia, may have their hair bobbed if they wish, but they must pay a tax for it. They are exempt up to 15 years of age, but after that there is a tax of 12 marks a year, with married women paying double. At

The Voice of History

Schoenau the tax is heavier, and other townships are preparing to follow the example of taxing shingled heads.[10]

Shanghai, Dec. 17.—The bobbed hair is considered the sign of a woman communist in China and at least fourteen bobbed girls and women have been shot by anti-red troops in Canton. During the ruthless campaign against the communists, troops shot down the girls and women in the streets without compunction.[11]

While the cutting of a woman's hair may seem a minor issue to people raised in a society where the practice is widely accepted, society is not the proper authority on this subject. God is the authority, and He has revealed His will on this matter through nature and through His Word. While an individual woman may not intend to violate God's plan when she cuts her hair, when the society as a whole abandons God's will in this matter the respective roles of men and women are blurred.

Regardless of what society may embrace from time to time, the Bible teaches that if a woman has long hair it is a glory to her, for it is given to her for a covering. The godly woman should be covered as a sign of submission to God's plan, and God has provided her with the natural covering of hair. On the other hand, the Bible teaches that if a woman cuts her hair or shaves her head, it is a disgrace to her in the sight of God.

Christian women who study this teaching of Scripture will have no desire to follow the leadership of the ungodly, the falsely liberated. Instead, they will desire to please the Lord and fulfill their God-given roles in life, realizing that only in this way will they find true joy.

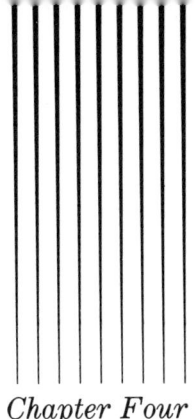

Chapter Four

Answers to Objections

In *Women's Hair—The Long and Short of It,* published in 1979, I responded to an unusual interpretation of I Corinthians 11:1-16 as it appeared in *Women's Adornment* by Ralph Woodrow. It seems necessary to analyze this position again since people who reject the teaching of I Corinthians 11 still refer to this view.[1] This chapter will identify the major objections and offer a response.

- *Objection: Paul had long hair at Corinth.*[2]

Answer: There is no doubt that I Corinthians 11 means that it is a shame for a man to have long hair. Verse 14 says, "If a man have long hair, it is a shame unto him."

Paul did not have long hair while at Corinth. It is true that he took a vow, and during the time of the vow he did not cut his hair (Acts 18:18). But in the context of I Corinthians 11, long hair is hair that has been allowed to grow; it is hair that has not been cut. Paul must have been in the practice of regularly cutting his hair, or else his abstention from cutting it for a period of time would not have been worthy of mention. What Paul did was unusual, out of the ordinary. He was in the regular practice of having his hair cut, and he did not allow it to grow as women did.

- *Objection: Part of I Corinthians 11 may not be Paul's words but the quotation of a letter from the Corinthians.*[3]

Answer: This objection is an awkward attempt to explain away the clear meaning of the passage. No serious scholar has adopted this view. It is dangerous to categorize a portion of the eternal Word of God as uninspired opinions of fallible men, especially in order to avoid the clear teaching of that passage.

A number of the objections are offered in an attempt to argue that part of I Corinthians 11 is not valid because it supposedly contradicts the rest of Scripture. Let us examine these objections individually.

- *Objection: Nothing else in the Bible indicates that a man should not cover his head while praying or prophesying. To the contrary, the high priest in the Old Testament was to cover his head as he ministered.* (See Leviticus 8:9, 13; 10:6; 21:10.)[4]

Answer: We have already seen that the covering mentioned in I Corinthians 11 is long hair itself, not a covering of cloth. Nevertheless, let us examine the scriptural references given.

First, we will look at Leviticus 21:10 in context: "And he that is the high priest among his brethren, upon whose head the anointing oil was poured, and that is consecrated to put on the garments, shall not uncover his head, nor rend his clothes; neither shall he go in to any dead body, nor defile himself for his father, or for his mother; neither

Answers to Objections

shall he go out of the sanctuary, nor profane the sanctuary of his God; for the crown of the anointing oil of his God is upon him: I am the LORD. And he shall take a wife in her virginity. A widow, or a divorced woman, or profane, or an harlot, these shall he not take: but he shall take a virgin of his own people to wife" (Leviticus 21:10-14).

This passage deals specifically with the requirements God had for the high priest. It does not speak to the issue of what was proper for the vast majority of Hebrew men. God had special expectations and demands of those in the priesthood. We may not know all the reasons for His requirements, but it is sufficient to know that God had a purpose. It would be a mistake, however, to say that what was required of the high priest was the norm. If this passage taught that the high priest should not uncover his head when he ministered, it would still have no bearing on the issue at hand, that is, whether a New Testament Christian male should pray and prophesy with an uncovered head.

But Leviticus 21:10 may not teach that the high priest could not minister unless he had an artificial covering on his head. The Hebrew word *para,* translated "uncover," carries the meaning "to loosen, to disorder, to disarrange." Some Bible translations render the word in such a way as to suggest that the issue was the priest's hair, not another covering: "The high priest . . . must not let his hair become unkempt" (NIV). "But he who is the high priest . . . shall not let the hair of his head hang loose" (Amplified).

The same Hebrew word is used in II Samuel 6:20: "Then David returned to bless his household. And Michal

Hair Length in the Bible

the daughter of Saul came out to meet David, and said, How glorious was the king of Israel to day, who uncovered himself to day in the eyes of the handmaids of his servants, as one of the vain fellows shamelessly uncovereth himself." This "uncovering" seems to speak specifically of David's actions in leaping and dancing before the Lord (II Samuel 6:16). That is, in Michal's opinion, David acted in a disorderly way. It is not a reference to removing his clothing, for David was dressed in a linen ephod, which was priestly attire (II Samuel 6:14).

It is doubtful that Leviticus 21:10 can be used to prove conclusively that the priests were commanded to wear an artificial head covering when ministering. Instead, the command seems to have to do with the proper care of their hair; they were not to be disheveled or unkempt.

From Leviticus 8:9, 13; 10:6 it appears that Aaron and his sons wore a type of headdress during their rituals, but again, what was commanded for the priesthood was not necessarily the broad practice among the Israelites. It would be wrong to use these verses of Scripture to say that, as a general rule, God approved of men covering their heads with veils when they engaged in spiritual exercises.

Leviticus 8:9 reads, "And he put the mitre upon his head; also upon the mitre, even upon his forefront, did he put the golden plate, the holy crown; as the LORD commanded Moses." The "mitre" was certainly not a veil, but a sort of turban.[5] A turban does not hang down as does a veil, but it covers essentially what a hat does.

Leviticus 8:13 reads, "And Moses brought Aaron's sons, and put coats upon them, and girded them with girdles, and put bonnets upon them; as the LORD com-

Answers to Objections

manded Moses." The "bonnets" were headbands, hardly the equivalent of a veil.[6] These verses do not prove that God is pleased with men veiling themselves when they pray or prophesy.

Leviticus 10:6 uses the same Hebrew word, *para*, as Leviticus 21:10. Thus, none of the verses cited prove anything about I Corinthians 11.

• *Objection: It was not wrong for Ezekiel, Moses, Elijah, and David to pray or prophesy with something on their heads.*[7] (See Ezekiel 24:15-21; Exodus 34:32-33; I Kings 19:13; II Samuel 15:30-32.)

Answer: Again, it is important to understand that I Corinthians 11 teaches that men are not to have a covering of long hair. Nevertheless, let us examine each of the Old Testament passages cited to see if wearing even a covering of cloth was typical or appropriate when praying or prophesying.

In Ezekiel 24:15-24, God told Ezekiel to bind a "tire" (an ornamental headdress) on his head. A study of the entire passage reveals that this action was a sign to the Israelites, an object lesson. What Ezekiel did was highly unusual, prompting the Israelites to say, "Wilt thou not tell us what these things are to us, that thou doest so?" (Ezekiel 24:19). We should also note the crisis nature of this story: Ezekiel's wife died, but instead of mourning, he went about as if nothing had happened!

This passage does not establish that it is pleasing to God for a man to veil himself when praying or prophesying. Rather, it demonstrates something that varies from the norm, something highly uncommon. Rather than proving that it was normal for a prophet to minister with his head covered, the passage proves just the opposite.

Hair Length in the Bible

In Exodus 34:29-33 Moses came down from Mt. Sinai with his face shining. And until he finished speaking with the Israelites he put a veil on his face. Again, this event was highly unusual and extraordinary, and it is doubtful whether Moses' talk with the Israelites was "prophecy." Moreover, Exodus 34:34 explicitly states, "But when Moses went in before the LORD to speak with him, he took the vail off, until he came out."

Elijah "wrapped his face in his mantle" when he talked to the Lord at Horeb (I Kings 19:13). A study of I Kings 19 reveals that this was a unique event in the life of Elijah. He was running in fear from Jezebel, who had threatened his life. Even though he had recently been used of the Lord to work a miracle on Mount Carmel, he despaired for his life, and he even prayed that he might die. His fear and lack of faith displeased the Lord, as is evident from God's question, "What doest thou here, Elijah?" (I Kings 19:9). God had not told him to flee from Jezebel; Elijah had acted on his own. The prophet attempted to justify his flight, whereupon God commanded him, "Go forth, and stand upon the mount before the LORD" (I Kings 19:11). There followed a strong wind, which rent the mountains and broke the rocks in pieces. Next there was an earthquake, followed by a fire. Finally, the Lord spoke in a still, small voice.

By this time, Elijah must have sensed the displeasure of God with his desertion from the scene of action. so when he went to stand before the Lord, he wrapped his face in his mantle. Apparently he did so as a sign of the shame he felt. Elijah had nothing to cover his face with except the mantle. He was not in the habit of covering his face when he talked with the Lord, or he would have had something more appropriate with which to do it. The mantle was not normally used for such a purpose. It was a makeshift covering, adapted on the spur of the moment because of the emotions of guilt and shame sweeping over Elijah because of his lack of faith.

When David fled from Absalom, he and the people with him went up Mt. Olivet weeping, with their heads covered (II Samuel 15:30). When someone told him that his counselor Ahithophel was one of the conspirators, David prayed that the Lord would turn his counsel into foolishness (II Samuel 15:31).

Again we see a very unusual situation. David and the men with him were in humiliation and mourning, for his son Absalom was attempting to overthrow him. David wept, went barefoot, and covered his head, all of which were signs of humiliation and shame. When he arrived at the top of the mount, Hushai the Archite came to meet him with his coat torn and earth upon his head. The highly emotional nature of this scene shows that these were things David did not normally do. He did not usually weep, go barefoot, and cover his head. It was not common for men like Hushai to go about with dirt on their heads. While it was not wrong for David to pray with his head covered, neither was it normal.

- *Objection: The men of Jerusalem and Judah "covered their heads" (Jeremiah 14:3), and modern Jews at prayer cover their heads with a shawl or a skullcap.*[8]

Answer: It is a mistake to try to determine the will of God by observing the practices of modern Jews. "Blindness in part is happened to Israel" (Romans 11:25). "But their minds were blinded: for until this day remaineth the same vail untaken away in the reading of the old testa-

Hair Length in the Bible

ment; which vail is done away in Christ" (II Corinthians 3:14). The modern practice of Jews covering their heads when they pray is without scriptural support. The men in Jeremiah 14:3 covered their heads in humiliation and distress: "And their nobles have sent their little ones to the waters: they came to the pits, and found no water; they returned with their vessels empty; they were ashamed and confounded, and covered their heads."

- *Objection: The questions in I Corinthians 11:13-14 can be translated as statements meaning it is proper for a woman to pray without a covering and that nature does not teach it to be shameful for a man to have long hair.*[9]

This proposed translation would break the unity of the passage, for earlier verses say that it is a shame for a woman's head to be shorn, shaved, or uncovered and that it is a shame for a man's head to be covered. No major Bible translation adopts the proposed translation, which would actually reverse the true meaning.

Verses 14 and 15 make use of the *men . . . de* conjunction, which is used in contrasting statements, meaning "on the one hand" and "on the other hand." In this case *men . . .de* is translated by "but" in verse 15. Thus, the *men* in verse 14 and the *de* in verse 15 tie the two verses together in contrast. The proposed translation for verses 13-14, however, would make the contrast with verse 15 meaningless.

In both verses 14 and 15, the mood of the verb *koma* ("have long hair") is subjunctive, signifying action that has the potential of taking place, and each verse shows the consequence of the contemplated action: If a man wears his hair long, then it is a shame to him (verse 14).

Answers to Objections

On the other hand, if a woman wears her hair long, then it is a glory to her (verse 15). And every translation preserves this meaning. The textual evidence and scholarship over the centuries unanimously affirm that verses 13-14 are in the form of two questions: "Is it proper . . . ?" and "Does not even nature itself teach you . . . ?" Every translation renders these two phrases as questions, and every Greek text includes the Greek equivalent of two question marks. It would be a great mistake to throw all of this evidence away and ignore the providential work of God in preserving His Word, in an attempt to support a questionable interpretation.

• *Objection: When we appeal to nature, the hair of both men and women will grow long if not cut.*

Answer: As I Corinthians 11:14 states, we do indeed learn a lesson from nature—instinct, or the natural course of things—about the proper length of hair on men and women. As a general rule, women in the Scriptures did not cut their hair, while men did cut their hair. In virtually every society of the world for thousands of years, it has been considered proper for men to cut their hair and for women to leave theirs uncut. While this basic principle has been violated from time to time, the violation has been the exception which proved the rule. While a man may grow his hair as long as that of a woman, historically this practice has not been widespread.

• *Objection: Absalom had long hair, and it was not considered shameful.*[10]

Answer: Absalom is not an example to follow. He was a rebel in every sense of the word. He attempted to overthrow his father's kingdom and brought great shame upon

Hair Length in the Bible

David. Elizabeth Rice Handford, an independent Baptist, answers this objection well:

> How short is short hair for a man? Evidently, short enough that there is no question that he is a man, not a woman. Absalom, the son of King David who tried to wrest the kingdom from his aged father, was a real rebel. His long hair was his pride and a symbol of his rebellion. He cut it once a year (II Sam. 14:26) and that evidently was not often enough. In the civil war that followed Absalom's seizing of the throne, Absalom was defeated. He fled on a mule, but his head caught in the thick boughs of a great oak (II Sam. 18:9). The mule ran on, leaving Absalom to hang until the leader of David's army found him and killed him. It seems probable that Absalom's long, luxuriant hair tangled in the tree branches. God evidently used Absalom's hair, the manifestation of his rebellion, to cause his death.[11]

Men in ancient times sometimes had hair that would be considered somewhat long by today's standards. But their hair was noticeably shorter than that of the women of their times. They did not have long hair according to the definition of I Corinthians 11, for as a general rule men in various cultures and times have cut their hair with at least some degree of frequency. Even Absalom cut his hair once a year.

- *Objection: If it was a shame for a man to have long hair, why were the Nazarites—men especially dedicated to God—required not to cut their hair?*[12]

Answer: Elizabeth Handford has offered a sound and thorough response:

Answers to Objections

Some confusion about long hair for men arises because of the instructions concerning the Nazarite vow in Numbers 6. A man (or woman) setting himself apart for the Lord could make a vow for a specific time. At the end of that time he was to bring an offering to the Tabernacle, and shave his head to show that the vow had been fulfilled. It was made for a specific number of days (Num. 6:13). We know of only three men in all Bible history who were Nazarites for their whole lives (Samuel, Samson, and John the Baptist). That seems to have been an uncommon, God-determined decision. Since I Corinthians 11:14 tells us it is a shame for a man to have long hair, this vow not only set a man apart, but also shamed him, perhaps signifying the shame Jesus endured (Heb. 13:13). It's obvious that these Nazarite men were not showing rebellion like the anarchist Jerry Rubin advocates. Jerry Rubin said: "Young kids, identify short hair with authority, discipline, unhappiness, boredom, hatred of life and long hair with letting go. Wherever we go our hair tells people where we stand on Vietnam, Wallace, campus disruption and drugs. We are living TV commercials for the revolution. Long hair is the beginning of our liberation from sexual oppression."[13]

- *Objection: When the Bible says it is a shame for a woman to be "shorn," it means to cut the hair off completely, to the scalp.*[14]

Answer: The word *shorn* is the past participle of *shear*. The word *shear* simply means "to cut," without specifying how much. (See the comments on I Corinthians

Hair Length in the Bible

11:6 in chapter 2.) When a piece of cloth is shorn by a person using a pair of shears, it is shorn regardless of how much is cut off.

According to I Corinthians 11, it is a shame for a woman to be shorn, or to have her hair cut. The chapter also says that her long hair (her uncut hair, hair which she has allowed to grow) is a glory to her. This teaching is still true today, for the Word of God does not change with fashions and fads.

• *Objection: A woman's shaved head was a shame at Corinth because of its association with cult prostitution, but it was not necessarily a sign of shame elsewhere. Instead, it was a common sign of mourning.*[15] (See Ezra 9:3; Isaiah 3:24; 15:2; 22:12; Jeremiah 7:29; 16:6; 48:37; Ezekiel 27:31; Amos 8:10; Micah 1:16.)

Answer: Most of the cited verses refer to men, not women. Many of the verses are written in a dramatic, poetical style, not necessarily speaking of literal baldness or shaving but of the shame which accompanies such action. They have reference to the judgment of God coming upon the disobedient.

Isaiah 3:24 speaks particularly of women, but the context of Isaiah 3:16-26, especially verse 17, shows that the baldness to come upon these women was the result of the scathing judgment of God.

• *Objection: If a soldier of Israel took a wife from among the captives of war, her head was to be shaved.*[16] (See Deuteronomy 21:10-14.)

Answer: This passage gives instructions for a Hebrew man taking a non-Hebrew wife from among the captives of war. There had to be a complete repudiation of her past. She had to become, in a sense, a new woman. This proc-

Answers to Objections

ess included shaving her head, paring her nails, discarding her old clothing, and mourning for her mother and father as if they were dead. She was to begin a new life, almost as if—in a limited sense—she were being reborn. If after all of this preparation, however, the man decided that he did not want her, he was to let her go wherever she wanted. He was not to sell her for money, because he had humbled her. The shaving of the head was part of the process of humiliation. Thus, this passage of Scripture gives no support for the idea that it is acceptable for Christian women to cut their hair.

- *Objection: Long hair piled on a woman's head can cause headaches.*[17]

Answer: A woman does not have to pile her hair on the top of her head. Many simple hairdos can alleviate this problem. Moreover, the Bible does teach the doctrine of healing. God will surely help a sincere Christian woman who has a problem of this nature.

- *Objection: Women who have long hair usually wear it on their heads in such a way that it covers little more than a man's short hair does.*[18]

Answer: A woman's hair is a symbolic or spiritual covering. Moreover, the Bible does not tell a Christian woman that she must style her hair in a certain way. Since women's hair naturally grows to different lengths, it is clear that its scriptural significance as a covering does not depend on whether it covers the ears, neck, shoulders, or back. A woman whose hair will not grow past her shoulders would be unable to meet the requirement if her hair must cover her back. But the outward symbol of uncut hair, however long, is to confirm the inward reality of a woman's spiritual condition in submitting to God's

Hair Length in the Bible

plan. It makes no difference how a woman's hair is styled unless it is extremely elaborate, distracting, or an expression of pride. (See I Timothy 2:9; I Peter 3:3.) Some people have suggested that a woman should fix her hair up or bind it to her head. That is, she should not permit it to hang down. These people commonly appeal to the description of the jealousy trial in Numbers 5:18: "And the priest shall set the woman before the LORD, and uncover the woman's head, and put the offering of memorial in her hands, which is the jealousy offering: and the priest shall have in his hand the bitter water that causeth the curse."

In this passage, the Hebrew word for "uncover" is *para*, which can mean "to unloose." Thus, some suppose that Hebrew women ordinarily bound their hair to their head and that this practice symbolized their being bound to their husbands. Some even appeal to Tertullian, who suggested that a woman's long, flowing hair has sexual attraction, an attraction that may have caused some angels to fall.

This view seems unlikely, however, because other verses use the Hebrew word *para* with reference to men. Moses said to his sons, "Uncover not your heads, neither rend your clothes; lest ye die" (Leviticus 10:6). The high priest was not to "uncover his head, nor rend his clothes" (Leviticus 21:10). If the reference to "uncovering" women's heads means that their hair was ordinarily bound to their heads in some way, the same would be true for men. But it is doubtful that anyone would suggest that a man should fasten his hair to his head with an artificial binding. To do so, he would have to have fairly long hair.

Instead, "uncovering" an accused woman's head ap-

Answers to Objections

parently referred simply to loosening her hair in the sense of disorderly disarrangement. This would have been a humbling experience for her, as was the entire trial. The Hebrew *para*, translated "uncover," can mean "to disorder, disarrange."[19]

The woman who washed the feet of Jesus with her tears and wiped them with her hair received no rebuke from Him (Luke 7:38). She could not have performed this ministry if her hair had been bound up on her head, and surely He would not have allowed her to perform a shameful or sinful act.

Tertullian's comments on many subjects are extremely fanciful, and neither he nor any other man is a final authority on this issue. Only the Word of God itself is infallible, and the Bible nowhere requires a certain hairstyle for women.

• *Objection: If a woman cannot cut or trim her hair at all in order to have "long hair," then a man who has hair hanging down to his shoulders does not have "long hair" if he simply cuts a few inches off occasionally.*[20]

Answer: A man's hair is not long by the definition of I Corinthians 11 if he is in the habit of regularly having it cut. However, the intent of the passage is to distinguish men from women in outward appearance. Thus, a man's hair should be clearly and noticeably shorter than that of women in his culture. Moreover, in our society longer hair on men became a sign of rebellion in the sixties and seventies, and a Christian man will not want to be identified with such rejection of authority. (See the comments on I Corinthians 11:14 in chapter 2.)

• *Objection: If a woman had to have hair hanging down her back to please God, many women could not do*

Hair Length in the Bible

so, for their hair simply will not grow very long.[21]

The definition of long hair in I Corinthians 11 is uncut hair that is allowed to grow. However, a woman need not have hair hanging down her back in order to please God. Women's hair grows in varying lengths. But regardless of the length of a woman's hair in inches, it is long if it is uncut and allowed to grow.

In summary, I Corinthians 11:2-16 teaches that it is a shame for a woman to have her hair shorn (cut), that it is a dishonor for her to pray with her head uncovered, that long hair is given to her for a covering, and that long hair is a glory to her. The same passage teaches that it is a dishonor for a man to pray with his head covered; specifically, it is a shame for him to have long hair. And these teachings are the commands of God, for in I Corinthians 14:37 Paul declared, "If any man think himself to be a prophet, or spiritual, let him acknowledge that the things that I write unto you are the commandments of the Lord."

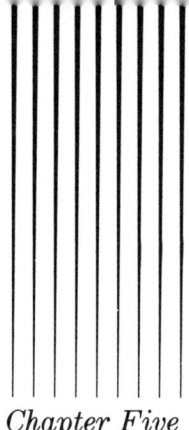

Chapter Five

The Letter and the Spirit

As chapter 4 has indicated, many people offer objections to the teachings of I Corinthians 11:2-16. Some women insist that they look younger and prettier with shorter hair. Others complain about the amount of time required to care for long hair. Some cut their hair on the ground that cutting it will cause it to grow better. Still others will not cut their hair, but will singe it or try to discover other ways to shorten it deliberately without disobeying the letter. At least one writer has suggested that I Corinthians 11:4-10 are not the inspired words of Paul at all, but were merely quoted from the Corinthians' letter to Paul, and he has appealed to somewhat obscure verses of Scripture in an effort to prove that I Corinthians 11:2-16 is out of harmony with the rest of the Word of God.

But when people make up their minds to be obedient to the Lord, no matter what the cost and regardless of current fads and fashions, they enjoy a peace and contentment that is absent when someone tries to find a way

Hair Length in the Bible

around His commandments.

To those women who insist they are more attractive with short hair, we ask, "To whom?" Elizabeth Handford comments in this regard:

> Surely not prettier to God, when He commanded long hair. Surely short hair is not prettier in the eyes of the woman who wants to please the Lord. Perhaps short hair is prettier by the world's standards. If so, we need to educate our hearts not to let the world set our standard of beauty for us.[1]

Elizabeth Handford also offers a woman's response to those who complain about the time and effort required to care for long hair:

> "Short hair is easier to care for than long hair is," another friend objects. They may be true, though I could build a fair case the other way, noting how many hours a week some hair-dos cost my friends. But again, let's ask ourselves, "Does the child of God ever make any choice simply on the basis of what is easy?" ... So I don't make any guarantees that long hair will be easier to care for, more attractive, or healthier. I just say that when a woman sets out to please the Lord, then she has His ear when she comes to pray.[2]

While some maintain that cutting the hair will cause it to grow better, ultimately how someone's hair grows is determined by nature and the God of nature. Similarly, Jesus said we cannot add to our height by taking thought for it, or worrying about it (Matthew 6:27). The growth

The Letter and the Spirit

of the hair is like the growth of any part of the body. It is in the hands of God. If a woman genuinely desires longer hair, she should pray for it. Moreover, it is not true that hair grows better if it is cut. Hair grows from the root. The *World Book Encyclopedia* describes this process:

> Hair grows by forming new cells at the base of the root. As new cells form around the nourishing papilla, the old ones are pushed away and die. The new cells gradually force the rod of dead cells up out of the follicle. Thus, old cells from the root become part of the shaft. . . . Hair continues to grow as long as the papilla provides nourishment for new cells. The papilla may remain active from weeks to years. . . . A hair of the human scalp usually grows about half an inch each month for two to four years. Then it falls out and a new hair replaces it. . . . After the old hair falls out, the papilla again becomes active and a new hair appears. Many factors, including age, diet, general health, and the condition of the skin, influence the activity of the papilla. Climate and seasonal change also affect the production of hair.[3]

The Bible does not contradict itself. It gives a consistent, clear testimony. When we study the subject of hair length in the Bible and read books on the subject, it is important to examine the entire context of each relevant Scripture reference. In doing so, we will be able to understand what the Bible teaches.

A person's attitude and spirit must be right with God. It does no good to pretend to obey God in external things

Hair Length in the Bible

only to harbor bitterness and judgmentalism. The Lord Jesus did not come into the world to condemn but to offer love and hope (John 3:17). The message that God has committed to us is the word of reconciliation (II Corinthians 5:19). Everyone will answer to God for himself; we are forbidden to judge one another's heart and motives (Matthew 7:1-5). Thus, the scriptural teaching on hair should not be used to condemn or belittle anyone but rather to inspire people to fulfill the will of God.

Hair length itself is simply a symbol. Christians must not merely fulfill the outward symbol; they must submit in reality to the plan of God and fulfill their respective roles. If they will do so, God will ensure that all things will work together for their good (Romans 8:28).

God desires obedience both inwardly and outwardly. It is His will for the external symbol to represent and be in harmony with the attitudes and behavior of Christians.

Notes

Chapter 1

[1] Since writing *Women's Hair—The Long and Short of It* in 1979, I have continued to do research on this subject. My discoveries include, but are not limited to, the following: Merle Ruth, *The Significance of the Christian Woman's Veiling* (Millersburg, OH: Calvary Publications, n.d.); William J. Martin in W. Ward Gasque and Ralph P. Martin, eds., *Apostolic History and the Gospel* (Grand Rapids, MI: William B. Eerdmans Publishing Company, 1970), pp. 231-41; R. K. Campbell, *Headship and Head Covering* (Sunbury, PA: Believers Bookshelf, n.d.); Bruce K. Waltke, "I Corinthians 11:2-16: An Interpretation," *Bibliotheca Sacra* 537 (1978): 46-57; David K. Lowery, "The Head Covering and the Lord's Supper in I Corinthians 11:2-34," *Bibliotheca Sacra* 570 (1986): 155-163; Wayne Grundun, "Does *Kephale* ('Head') Mean 'Source' or 'Authority Over' in Greek Literature? A Survey of 2,336 Examples," *Trinity Journal* 6 New Series (Spring 1985): 38-59; D. A. Carson, *Exegetical Fallacies* (Grand Rapids, MI: Baker Book House, 1984), pp. 36-40, 98, 99, 120, 141; Gregory H. Pope, *No Greater Burden* (N.p.: JM Publications, 1985); David K. Bernard, *Practical Holiness: A Second Look* (Hazelwood, MO: Word Aflame Press, 1985), pp. 209-223; and several works published privately by the authors.

[2] David K. Lowery in John F. Walvoord and Roy B. Zuck, eds., *The Bible Knowledge Commentary, New Testament Edition* (Wheaton, IL: Victor Books, 1983), p. 517.

[3] W. Harold Mare in Frank E. Gaebelein, ed., *The Expositor's Bible Commentary*, (Grand Rapids, MI: Zondervan Publishing House, 1976), vol. 10, p. 226.

[4] Lowery, *Bible Knowledge Commentary*, p. 528.

[5] Martin, *Apostolic History*, p. 231.

Chapter 2
 [1] Carson, *Exegetical Fallacies,* p. 37. Indeed, Carson says that Berkeley and Alvera Mickelsen's attempt to interpret *kephale* in this passage as "source" or "origin" is an example of a word-study fallacy, the "appeal to unknown or unlikely meanings."
 [2] Lowery, *Bible Knowledge Commentary,* p. 529.
 [3] Mare, *Expositor's Bible Commentary* vol. 10, p. 257, n. 4. Brackets in original.
 [4] Lowery, *Bible Knowledge Commentary,* p. 529.
 [5] Martin, *Apostolic History,* p. 233.
 [6] Ibid.
 [7] Ruth, *Significance of the Christian Woman's Veiling,* pp. 8, 13.
 [8] Martin, *Apostolic History,* pp. 232-33.
 [9] H. D. M. Spence and Joseph S. Excell, eds., *The Pulpit Commentary* (Grand Rapids, MI: William B. Eerdmans Publishing Company, reprinted 1977), vol. 19, pp. 362, 370.
 [10] Lowery, *Bible Knowledge Commentary,* p. 529.
 [11] Bruce K. Waltke, "I Corinthians 11:2-16: An Interpretation," *Bibliotheca Sacra,* vol. 135 no. 537 (January-March 1978), p. 46.
 [12] Ibid., p. 50.
 [13] Ibid.
 [14] Ibid., p. 57.
 [15] Martin, *Apostolic History,* p. 233.
 [16] F. Wilbur Gingrich, *Shorter Lexicon of the Greek New Testament* (Chicago, IL: The University of Chicago Press, 1965), p. 114.
 [17] These include the Revised Standard Version, The New English Bible, The Holy Bible from Ancient Eastern Manuscripts, The New American Bible, New International Version, Amplified Bible, and A New Translation by James Moffatt. I do not necessarily endorse these translations but simply mention them to illustrate the meaning of the word *shorn.*

[18]Martin, *Apostolic History*, pp. 234-35.
[19]Ibid., pp. 238-39.
[20]Ibid., p. 238.
[21]*The Interpreter's Dictionary of the Bible*, vol. 4, p. 747.
[22]*The International Standard Bible Encyclopedia*, vol. 5, p. 3047.
[23]*The New Schaff-Herzog Encyclopedia of Religious Knowledge*, vol. 4, p. 4.
[24]Research by Paul Ferguson.
[25]Noah Webster, *An American Dictionary of the English Language* (New York: S. Converse, 1828), reprinted by the Foundation for American Christian Education, 1967, s.v. *for*.
[26]*The Pulpit Commentary*, vol. 19, p. 363.

Chapter 3
[1]*The New Schaff-Herzog Encyclopedia of Religious Knowledge*, vol. 5, p. 18.
[2]*The World Book Encyclopedia*, fiftieth anniversary edition, vol. 9, p. 11.
[3]Paul Kurtz, ed., *Humanist Manifestos I and II* (Buffalo, NY: Prometheus Books, 1973), pp. 15-16.
[4]*Saturday Review of Education*, March 1973.
[5]Karen Clark, Sandy Gerber, Nancy Lehmann, Susan Miler, and Helen Sullinger, *The Document: Declaration of Feminism* (Minneapolis: n.p., 1971), pp. 10-12, 16.
[6]*Tulsa Sunday World*, August 21, 1977.
[7]A. D. Urshan *The Witness of God* (Chicago, IL: n.p.), November 1927, p. 18.
[8]Ibid.
[9]*The Witness of God*, February 1928, p. 11.
[10]Ibid.
[11]Ibid., p. 12.

Chapter 4
[1]I was somewhat surprised to discover a book published in

1985 that leans heavily on Woodrow's work without any reference to my previous response. See Gregory H. Pope, *No Greater Burden* (N.p.: JM Publications, 1985).

[2] See Ralph Woodrow, *Women's Adornment* (Riverside, CA: n.p., 1976), p. 37.

[3] See ibid., p. 38.

[4] See ibid., p. 39.

[5] The word is rendered "turban" by the New International Version, the Amplified Bible, and Moffatt.

[6] The word is rendered "headbands" by the New International Version. The Revised Standard Version and Moffatt render it "caps."

[7] See Woodrow, *Women's Adornment*, pp. 39-40.

[8] See ibid., p. 40.

[9] See ibid., pp. 44-45.

[10] See ibid., p. 46.

[11] Elizabeth Rice Handford, *Your Clothes Say It for You* (Murfreesboro, TN: Sword of the Lord Publishers, 1976), p. 64.

[12] See Woodrow, *Women's Adornment*, p. 47.

[13] Handford, *Your Clothes Say It for You*, pp. 64-65.

[14] See Woodrow, *Women's Adornment*, p. 50.

[15] See ibid.

[16] See ibid., p. 51.

[17] See ibid., p. 52.

[18] See ibid.

[19] Aaron Pick, *Dictionary of Old Testament Words for English Readers* (Grand Rapids, MI: Kregel Publications, 1977), s.v. "uncover."

[20] See Woodrow, *Women's Adornment*, p. 52.

[21] See ibid., p. 53.

Chapter 5

[1] Handford, *Your Clothes Say It for You*, p. 66.

[2] Ibid., pp. 66-67.

[3] *World Book Encyclopedia*, vol. 9, p. 10.